OVERCOMING ADVERSITY:
SHARING THE AMERICAN DREAM

EVA LONGORIA

MASON CREST PUBLISHERS
PHILADELPHIA

OVERCOMING ADVERSITY:
SHARING THE AMERICAN DREAM

OVERCOMING ADVERSITY:
SHARING THE AMERICAN DREAM

EVA LONGORIA

MARY SCHULTE

MASON CREST PUBLISHERS
PHILADELPHIA

ABOUT CROSS-CURRENTS

When you see this logo, turn to the Cross-Currents section at the back of the book. The Cross-Currents features explore connections between people, places, events, and ideas.

Produced by OTTN Publishing, Stockton, New Jersey

Mason Crest Publishers
370 Reed Road
Broomall, PA 19008
www.masoncrest.com

First printing

1 3 5 7 9 8 6 4 2

Library of Congress Cataloging-in-Publication Data

Schulte, Mary, 1958-
  Eva Longoria / Mary Schulte.
      p. cm. — (Sharing the American dream : overcoming adversity)
  ISBN 978-1-4222-0595-2 (hardcover) — ISBN 978-1-4222-0754-3 (pbk.)
 1. Longoria, Eva, 1975- 2. Actors—United States—Biography—Juvenile literature. I. Title.
 PN2287.L6325S38 2008
 791.4502'8092—dc22
 [B]
                                    2008040022

OVERCOMING ADVERSITY:
SHARING THE AMERICAN DREAM

TABLE OF CONTENTS

CHAPTER ONE

A DREAM COME TRUE

For Eva Longoria, family has always been foremost. So it's not surprising that, when she appeared on *The Oprah Winfrey Show* on February 6, 2006, Eva revealed that her greatest dream in life had been to buy her parents a house. The vivacious brunette—who plays Gabrielle Solis on the TV series *Desperate Housewives*—wanted to return the blessings her parents, Ella and Enrique Longoria, had given her.

Humble Beginnings

Eva and her three older sisters had grown up on a ranch in Corpus Christi, Texas. Their father was a tool engineer. Their mother was a special education teacher. Ella Longoria had been motivated to choose that career because the oldest Longoria daughter, Elizabeth, was intellectually disabled.

The Longorias were poor. They lived on farmland that had been handed down through generations of the family. Eva's mother and father went without heat and air conditioning to provide money for cheerleading outfits and band instruments for their girls.

She and her sisters didn't realize they were poor, Eva would recall, because they were surrounded by love. The girls thought

Beautiful and talented, Eva Longoria has become one of the most popular TV stars in the United States.

it was great that they had a swimming pool on their property. They didn't know it was a watering trough for cows. Eva's family made the best of what they had, and she remembered her childhood as a time of love and laughter.

A New House

When the money started rolling in from her role as Gabrielle on the nighttime soap opera *Desperate Housewives*, Eva bought her parents a house in a beautiful neighborhood in San Antonio, Texas.

But Enrique and Ella Longoria had trouble overcoming their frugal ways and enjoying the new house. Eva asked Nate Berkus, a design consultant who appears on *The Oprah Winfrey Show*, to redecorate the house so that it would seem more comfortable for her parents. She wanted her parents to be surrounded by beautiful things.

READ MORE

For a primer on *Desperate Housewives*, turn to page 42.

She also wanted the home to reflect her family's Mexican heritage. Berkus accepted the challenge.

As they toured her parents' house, Eva pointed out items she thought needed to be changed. Her parents were using the outdoor wicker furniture that Eva gave them, but instead of having it outside on the patio, they used it for dining room furniture.

The hide from a deer her father had killed when he was younger hung on one wall. It was the one thing he insisted on bringing from the family ranch when they moved from Corpus Christi. That and his beta fish.

Eva and her mother shared the feeling that family is the most important thing to consider in a home. As Berkus walked through

Eva with her parents, Enrique and Ella Longoria, at the premiere of the 2008 movie *Over Her Dead Body*. The actress is very close to her parents.

the family room, he asked Ella Longoria what type of furniture she would like to have. A leather couch, she replied.

To understand the family's sense of style, Berkus asked what they considered beautiful. Enrique, Ella, and Eva Longoria all gave the same answer: color. As Eva explained, bold color goes with their Mexican culture.

Redecoration Accomplished

At the unveiling of his work—video of which was shown on *The Oprah Winfrey Show*—Nate Berkus escorted Eva and her parents through their beautifully redone home. Eva's first response was that she felt as if she were in Mexico. Berkus explained that the bright colors, the terra cotta tiles, and the pottery he had used are all elements of Mexican culture.

Eva could hardly contain her excitement. She squealed with delight when she saw some of the things Berkus had done. The look of astonishment on her mother's face when she saw the state-of-the-art appliances in the kitchen brought tears to Eva's eyes. "She's never had a dishwasher before," Eva said. Her mother had always washed dishes by hand for their family of six.

Eva hugged her parents. She humbly thanked them for all they had done for her.

A Surprise Visit

Back at the studio, Oprah Winfrey's viewers were in for a treat. Eva's boyfriend, San Antonio Spurs basketball star Tony Parker, strolled onto the set. The 6'2" point guard, who towers over the petite actress by a foot, obviously didn't mind as she snuggled up to his shoulder.

It was their first television interview together, and Oprah was fishing for details about their future plans. She asked how they met and what they thought of each other.

READ MORE

For a brief profile of Oprah Winfrey, see page 44.

Eva looks up to boyfriend Tony Parker at an ABC press event. Eva and Tony made their first television appearance together on *The Oprah Winfrey Show* in 2006.

Their first meeting happened in 2004, Eva said. She took her father to a Spurs game and they were invited to meet the players after the game. Eva had just returned from France and introduced herself in French to Tony, who was raised in Paris. He immediately began to speak French, but Eva couldn't understand him.

"Oh, no, no, no, that's all I know, my name!" she recalled saying.

Neither Eva nor Tony knew how big a star the other was. Tony had never watched *Desperate Housewives*. So when they met at an IHOP for breakfast a few days later, people came up to Tony and asked for an autograph. As fans noticed who was sitting with him, they were surprised. They immediately turned to ask Eva for an autograph, too.

"And he's like, 'Why is everybody asking for your autograph?'" Eva told Oprah with a laugh. "So I had to explain to him. *Desperate Housewives* isn't an easy thing to explain!"

Explaining the scheming Gabrielle Solis may be difficult. But it's easy to figure out where Eva got her values, her playful sense of humor, and her tremendous work ethic: her family and her Mexican-American culture.

CHAPTER TWO

POOR BUT HAPPY

Eva Jacqueline Longoria was born on March 15, 1975, in Corpus Christi, Texas. Her parents, Ella Eva Mireles Longoria and Enrique Longoria Jr., are both native Texans of Mexican descent. Records show that Eva's great-great grandfather, Ponciano Longoria, came to the United States from Mexico in 1859 when he was six years old.

Eva, the youngest of four girls whose initials are all E. J., used to wonder if she was adopted. She had dark hair and dark skin, while her three sisters—Elizabeth Judina, Emily Jeannette, and Esmeralda Josephina—all had lighter hair and fairer skin. Her sisters jokingly called Eva *la prieta fea*, which means "the ugly, dark one."

Lessons from the Family

The oldest daughter, Elizabeth—called Liza by the family—was mentally handicapped. Doctors said she would never walk or talk or have a normal life. Eva's mother was determined that her daughter would have a good life no matter what was required. She took over Liza's care and became a special education teacher so she could accompany her daughter to school.

"My first memories as a kid were volunteering with the Special Olympics," Eva told an interviewer in 2007. "Growing up with a sister with special needs makes you selfless. When you have that mentality, you do think of others first. Our culture in general is a very giving and helpful community."

Eva often says that her mother's remarkable determination has inspired her throughout her life. In addition to caring for Liza, Ella Longoria worked a full-time job and shuttled her daughters to their activities.

"I grew up in a household of women—aunts, sisters, a house full of strong female role models," Eva said in *Texas Monthly*. "For me, there is nothing I can do that compares to what my mom did. I'm a great multi-tasker because of her."

Eva (white dress) with her mother and two of her three older sisters. When she was young, Eva was considered the ugly duckling of the family.

Eva also learned much from her father. Enrique Longoria was a rancher and hunter, and he taught Eva and her sisters how to handle a gun and how to skin a deer. Eva began hunting with her father when she was six, and she still hunts with him on occasion. "I could skin a deer, I could skin a pig. I can pluck a quail—you name it, I've done it," Eva told Stone Phillips of *Dateline NBC*.

READ MORE

For Latina girls, the *quinceañera* is a major rite of passage. Page 45 has details.

Although Eva's father worked long hours as a tool engineer at an army depot, and her mother taught special education, the Longorias had little money to spare. When she was 12, Eva realized her family wouldn't have enough money for her *quinceañera*. But she was determined to have the traditional Latina coming-of-age celebration. So she swiped her sister's ID and got a job flipping burgers at a Wendy's restaurant. Money Eva earned helped pay for her party when she turned 15. She wore a dress that her mother found at a flea market, and the party was held at the local Elk's Lodge.

From Ugly Duckling to Beauty Pageant Winner

Describing herself as a young child, Eva told *Dateline NBC* that she was all skin and bones. "I was clumsy. I was dark. I was ugly. So I think growing up, I didn't depend on looks or the superficiality of being pretty because I wasn't. I always knew that I'm gonna have to work hard. Nothing's gonna be given to me. And I think that comes from my mom and dad."

Eva overcame her early clumsiness to become a good athlete. She was on school basketball, track, and gymnastics teams.

She also worked hard to make the cheerleading squad at Roy Miller High School in Corpus Christi. That led to a cheerleading scholarship at Texas A&M University–Kingsville, where she majored in kinesiology (the study of human movement). To pay for her college expenses, Eva worked six jobs, including dental assistant and basketball referee.

Beauty pageants were another way for Eva to earn extra money in college. She may have considered herself unattractive as a child, but at the age of 18, she won her first beauty

Eva in her uniform as the head drum major at Roy Miller High School in Corpus Christi, Texas. In addition to leading the marching band, Eva, a good athlete, played several sports.

pageant competition. Five years later, she was crowned Miss Corpus Christi USA. Part of the prize was a trip to Los Angeles to compete in a modeling and talent competition sponsored by the International Modeling and Talent Agency (IMTA). After watching Eva at the IMTA program, 38 agencies and managers wanted to represent her.

Eva's plan had been to get an undergraduate degree and a master's degree, then to work in sports medicine or athletic training. But she began to rethink that plan. After graduating from college with a bachelor's degree in kinesiology, Eva signed with a theatrical agent and moved to Hollywood to pursue an acting career.

Becoming an Actress

Although she had an agent, producers didn't exactly knock down the door to offer Eva parts. She worked for three years as a headhunter for an executive search firm before her acting career began to take off.

When she first arrived in Hollywood, Eva had set her sights on acting in a soap opera, since that was her family's favorite type of show. "I took soap technique classes, I took soap opera acting classes, I took soap opera makeup classes—I took anything that has to do with a soap," she confessed to NBC's Stone Phillips. "Believe me, I could do a movie with Al Pacino and it still won't be as great to my family as when I had one line on " 'General Hospital.' "

Eva's one-line role in a *General Hospital* episode came in 2000. The same year, she appeared in a single episode of *Beverly Hills, 90210*.

In February 2001, Eva landed a meatier part. She played a crazy woman named Isabella Braña Williams on the daytime soap opera *The Young and the Restless*. Eva portrayed the murderous Isabella until August 2003, when the character was sent to a mental institution and written out of the show.

Eva's two and a half years on *The Young and the Restless* was enough to get her a prime-time role as Detective Gloria Duran on *L.A. Dragnet*. Eva was already careful about the roles she accepted, conscious of the image she would project as a Latina. "My role on *L.A. Dragnet*," she told an inter-viewer, "was as a tough, smart, sexy cop, and that was a very positive role that I played and a positive image that I represented."

READ MORE

For some information about the popular soap opera *The Young and the Restless*, turn to page 46.

The cast of *L.A. Dragnet*. The short-lived crime series starred Ed O'Neill (second from right). Eva Longoria (second from left) played Latina detective Gloria Duran in 10 episodes.

Unfortunately, the show ran for just one season, 2003–04.

Hollywood Love Life

By this time, Eva's personal life was a ripe subject for gossip. In January 2002, she had eloped and married a fellow actor, Tyler Christopher, in Las Vegas. Christopher was a star on *General Hospital*. The marriage lasted only two years.

"You get through it," Eva said of her failed marriage. "My philosophy was that every time a door closed, I knew one would open."

Doors to romance did open soon after Eva's divorce. At the 2004 Emmy Awards and the 2004 American Music Awards, she was seen on the red carpet with JC Chasez of the pop group 'N Sync. She also was linked with actors Hayden Christensen and Mario Lopez.

Eva with JC Chasez of 'N Sync at the 2004 American Music Awards. The two dated after Eva's divorce from actor Tyler Christopher.

Eva's relationships would soon take a backseat to her career, however. She was about to become one of TV's most talked-about stars.

CHAPTER THREE

AMERICA'S FAVORITE HOUSEWIFE

In 2004, Eva Longoria auditioned for a part in an upcoming prime-time series. The show would be a satire of the soap opera genre. Called *Desperate Housewives,* it would follow sordid goings-on among a group of women living on affluent Wisteria Lane. And, at a time when the major television networks were pushing for diversity, the show would include some interesting—and unconventional—Latino characters. Eva's timing was ideal.

When Eva went to try out for the *Desperate Housewives* cast, it was her fifth audition of the day. She hadn't had time to read through the entire script. When director Marc Cherry asked Eva what she thought of the script, she confessed that she'd only read the part of Gabrielle Solis, the sultry gold digger. The director said he knew right then that Eva was perfect for the character "because it was such a Gabrielle thing to say."

Eva was offered a contract to star in *Desperate Housewives.* She signed on, joining costars Teri Hatcher, Felicity Huffman, Nicollette Sheridan, and Marcia Cross.

The show premiered on ABC on October 3, 2004. It was an immediate hit. Suddenly, Eva Longoria was a household name. Her character was especially popular among fellow Latinos. Eva

The stars of *Desperate Housewives*. From left: Eva Longoria, Felicity Huffman, Marcia Cross, Teri Hatcher, Nicollette Sheridan.

would later attribute much of that to the reversal of stereotypes that her role represented, which was also one of the reasons she enjoyed playing Gabrielle Solis. "Let me tell you what the Latinos are most proud of when the role of the Solises came out," Eva explained to *Dateline NBC*, "was that we were the most affluent on the block. We were the richest people on the block and that we had a white gardener."

If she loved playing Gabrielle on TV, Eva was quick to point out that she and her fictional character are very different. "She hates children and I want ten," Eva told an interviewer. "She married for money—I would never marry for money. She's materialistic, I'm not." Still, the actress did admit that she shares a few characteristics with Gabrielle Solis. "The things we have in common," she said, "are our ambition and our drive, and we want what we want when we want it. And I think I've been like that in my life."

Fateful Meeting

With the runaway success of *Desperate Housewives*, Eva Longoria had rocketed to fame by November 2004, when she and her father went to see a San Antonio Spurs basketball game. After the game, Eva and her dad were invited to meet the players. Eva wasn't really interested, but she accepted the invitation because her father is a big Spurs fan.

Point guard Tony Parker didn't know who Eva was, but when she walked into the room, he wanted to find out. He invited her and her father to dinner.

"I said her dad could come too, but I didn't mean it," Parker told *Sports Illustrated*. "Anyway, he didn't come, and Eva and I talked all night long."

Eva and Tony talked on the phone for a month before having their first official date in January 2005. They went public about their relationship at the Screen Actor's Guild Awards in February 2005.

Tony, who is seven years younger than Eva, was raised in Paris by his father, an American-born professional basketball player, and his mother, a Dutch model. In 2001, at the age of 19, Tony signed a contract to play with the San Antonio Spurs. By the time he met Eva Longoria, Tony had helped lead the Spurs to an NBA championship, in 2003.

Tony's basketball commitments and Eva's acting schedule forced them to settle for a long-distance relationship. But they never went more than two weeks without seeing each

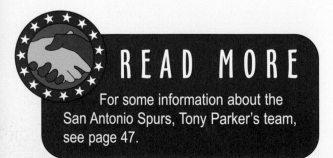

READ MORE

For some information about the San Antonio Spurs, Tony Parker's team, see page 47.

Eva and her boyfriend, Tony Parker, celebrate the San Antonio Spurs' 2005 NBA championship, June 25, 2005.

other during the season, piling on the frequent-flier miles and spending time together in San Antonio and Hollywood.

The Benefits and Costs of Fame

Being a star in the entertainment industry creates enormous opportunities but, as Eva Longoria quickly found out, also comes with some major drawbacks. On the one hand, Eva's newfound fame helped her land many lucrative endorsement contracts. In April 2005, for example, she signed a $1.9 million exclusive worldwide contract to be the face of the cosmetics company L'Oréal. On the other hand, everywhere Eva went, she was followed by the paparazzi, and her personal life—including her relationship with Tony Parker—became fodder for scores of tabloid magazines and Web sites.

In such circumstances, even minor incidents are often magnified and distorted. In 2005, an altercation between Eva and Tony and a bicycle patrolman made front-page headlines in San Antonio and was reported extensively in the tabloids. The incident occurred early in the morning on Christmas Eve. Tony's SUV was blocking traffic in front of a San Antonio nightclub that had refused the couple admission because Tony wasn't sufficiently dressed up. The

A celebrity photographer snapped this picture of Eva as she left a café in Los Angeles. Wherever Eva goes in public, a pack of paparazzi follow—one of the prices of Hollywood stardom.

policeman rapped on the hood of the SUV and ordered Tony to move the vehicle. Heated words were exchanged. According to the police report, Eva became furious and yelled that the officer was "just a Mexican bike cop" who wanted Tony's autograph. Eva denied the police officer's account, noting that she is a Mexican American herself and claiming she would never use ethnic slurs to put someone down. Later, it would be revealed that the police officer involved in the incident was under investigation for misconduct.

The public's hunger for gossip about Eva Longoria only increased. And, as many observers pointed out, Eva wasn't shy about discussing her personal life when asked by a reporter. During the fall of 2006, however, Eva tried to step out of the limelight for a while. In October, Tony Parker was spotted dancing with a former girlfriend at a party. The tabloids reported that Eva and Tony had split up. But behind the scenes, the couple recommitted to their relationship. Tony was in France to play a series of exhibition games, and Eva flew to Paris to be with him.

A month later, in November 2006, Tony secretly went to Eva's home in Los Angeles. He filled the house with rose petals and lit candles. When Eva arrived, Tony proposed to her. She accepted. America's favorite TV housewife was going to become a real-life wife.

CHAPTER FOUR

ROLE MODEL

Eva Longoria has always been proud of her Hispanic heritage, and with her success on *Desperate Housewives* she became one of the most visible Latinas in the United States. Eva was determined to use her fame to benefit Hispanics.

Over the years, Eva has given her time, her talent, and her money to a wide range of Latino organizations. These include the United Farm Workers (UFW), the Mexican American Legal Defense Educational Fund (MALDEF), the Dolores Huerta Foundation, and the National Council of La Raza (NCLR).

A Passion to Serve

Since her first years in Hollywood, Eva had been a volunteer for PADRES Contra El Cáncer. The California-based charity helps children with cancer and their families. While PADRES focuses on the Latino community, its programs are available to people of all races and ethnic origins. In 2005, Eva became the national spokesperson for PADRES. Two years later, she donated her salary from one episode of *Desperate Housewives* to the charity. That was a substantial sum—in 2007, the leads of the show renewed their contracts with ABC for four years at $440,000 per episode.

Eva with young cancer patients at a benefit gala for PADRES Contra El Cáncer, October 7, 2008. The actress, a big supporter of PADRES, became the group's national spokesperson in 2005.

"It's amazing how you feel when you help people," Eva noted. "Joy has an actual texture. You can feel it."

In 2006, Eva founded her own charitable organization, called Eva's Heroes. Though not connected with the Hispanic community, the organization was very close to Eva's heart. It provides services and programs to help developmentally challenged youth aged 14 to 21. Eva's inspiration in founding the charity was, of course, her big sister Liza, who graduated from high school and lives independently, despite her disabilities.

READ MORE

For additional information about Eva's Heroes, see page 48.

"Liza . . . was my hero growing up," Eva said. "It was a blessing to watch her overcome every obstacle—tying her shoes, putting on a shirt, getting out the front door. And yet she still had a job and would come home on the bus by herself and help with dinner. You could only imagine the hurdles she encountered every minute of the day."

Inspirations

If Liza was Eva's hero as she grew up, Eva also credits the examples of three other Latina women with making her the person she is. Her confidence, her moral center, and her work ethic, Eva says, can be traced to these three role models. The first was Dolores Huerta, a labor organizer who cofounded the United Farm Workers union with Cesar Chávez. Since the 1960s, the UFW has fought for the rights of migrant farm laborers, many of whom are Mexican or Mexican American. Today, Eva considers Huerta a close friend, and the two worked together to make a documentary about a day in the life of an immigrant farmworker. Eva herself spent a day in the fields for the film. She was shocked by what she saw. "It's horrendous.

[The migrant workers] are being treated like slaves," Eva told an interviewer.

Eva's second inspiration was Selena, a popular Tejano singer. Selena lived in Corpus Christi and performed concerts that the Longoria family attended. During the late 1980s and early 1990s, when there weren't many high-profile Latina entertainers in the United States, Selena showed Eva that perhaps she too might one day perform. Tragically, Selena's life was cut short in 1995, when she was murdered by the president of her fan club. The singer was only 23 years old.

Selena in concert, 1995. The Tejano singer was one of Eva Longoria's major inspirations when Eva was young.

Eva has said her mother, Ella, is her greatest inspiration. The two are seen here in a 2008 photo.

Perhaps Eva's most important inspiration was her mother. Eva credits her mom with always believing in her, which Eva says gave her the strength to believe in herself.

Just as the young Eva was motivated by the strong examples set by Dolores Huerta, by Selena, and by her mother, she believes it is important for her to be a good role model for girls today. "I take huge responsibility and I embrace it," Eva told an interviewer. "Growing up now, kids can be misguided because of the tabloids."

Opening Doors for Others

Helping others realize their potential is the essence of being a good role model. Much of this involves providing an example of success that a young person can relate to and emulate. Eva

Longoria is committed to ensuring that Latinos have role models. One way she has done this is through her work with the ALMA (American Latino Media Arts) Awards. Sponsored by the National Council of La Raza—the largest Hispanic civil rights and advocacy organization in the United States—the ALMA Awards celebrate Latino heritage and honor positive portrayals of Latinos in film and television.

In 2006, and again in 2007 and 2008, Eva served as host and producer of the prime-time ALMA Awards television broadcast. "She's not just a great actress," NCLR president and CEO Janet Murguía said of Eva, "but a great humanitarian. She's very committed to opening doors for Hispanics."

Eva's commitment to Latino issues and causes has been recognized by numerous organizations. The National Hispanic Foundation for the Arts, a group dedicated to the advancement of Latinos in the media, honored Eva with its Horizon Award in 2005. The following year, she received the Latina Visionary and Community Empowerment Award at the National Hispanic Women's Conference. In 2006, Eva's significant contributions to the empowerment of the Latino community were recognized by the National Hispana Leadership Institute. The institute presented Eva with its Chair's Award, which honors the woman of the year.

READ MORE

The ALMA Awards recognize positive portrayals of Latinos in the media. To learn more, turn to page 49.

On the Big Screen

Between *Desperate Housewives*, her work with charities, and her promotion of Latino causes—to say nothing of plans for her upcoming wedding—Eva Longoria was a very busy person. But

Eva Longoria hosts the 2008 ALMA Awards, held August 17 at the Pasadena Civic Auditorium in Pasadena, California.

in 2006, she found time to try to get her motion picture career off the ground.

Many actors who make it big on television set their sights on a movie career, and Eva was no exception. But making the transition from the little screen to the big screen can be difficult. Achieving stardom on a TV series is no guarantee of success in motion pictures, as Eva would discover.

Eva's first films—*Carlita's Secret* (2004), *Hustler's Instinct* (2005), and *Harsh Times* (2005)—had been flops. Unlike those movies, however, 2006's *The Sentinel* featured a cast of established stars, including Michael Douglas, Kiefer Sutherland, and Kim Basinger. In the political thriller, a traitor within the ranks of the Secret Service plots to assassinate the president of the United States. Eva, playing a young Secret Service agent, becomes involved in unraveling the assassination plot.

Despite its big-name cast, *The Sentinel* did poorly at the box office and was widely panned by the critics. Stephen Holden of the *New York Times* summed up the view of many critics. Holden called the film "deeply ridiculous, suspense-free, and potentially career-damaging" for its stars.

Even as her movie career foundered, however, Eva Longoria remained one of TV's biggest stars. And her celebrity would only increase with her marriage to a pro sports hero.

CHAPTER FIVE

"I LOVE LIFE"

Saturday, July 7, 2007, dawned chilly and overcast in Paris. By afternoon, however, the sun pierced through the clouds. It was an auspicious sign for Eva Longoria and Tony Parker. This was their wedding day.

The couple exchanged vows at the Eglise Saint-Germain l'Auxerrois, a church located near the Louvre Museum. Saint-Germain was built between the 12th and 15th centuries. Before the ceremony, a large crowd gathered outside the church, hoping to catch a glimpse of the many celebrities among the 250 or so invited guests. But guards held large black umbrellas to prevent the paparazzi from photographing guests, who included Tony's San Antonio Spurs teammates; Eva's *Desperate Housewives* costars Teri Hatcher, Felicity Huffman, and Nicollette Sheridan; and other big-name entertainers, such as Michael Douglas, Catherine Zeta-Jones, Sheryl Crow, and Jessica Alba.

Eva described her wedding as "quite simple, traditional and personal." The Roman Catholic ceremony incorporated elements of the bride's Mexican-American heritage and the groom's French background. Eva said her vows in French. Tony said his in English.

One day before their church wedding, Eva Longoria and Tony Parker got married in a civil service, as required by French law. In this photo, Eva waves to fans as she enters Paris's City Hall, where the civil service was performed on July 6, 2007.

If the wedding ceremony was simple, the wedding reception was anything but. Guests were transported in big red buses to the Vaux-le-Vicomte, a 17th-century chateau located 35 miles southeast of Paris. The castle has a marble-floored ballroom and chandelier-studded dining room. Even the wedding cake—made in the United States and flown to France for the occasion—was spectacular. The red, five-tiered vanilla-bean pound cake was filled with crushed organic raspberries and decorated with 500 handmade sugar flowers.

Vaux-le-Vicomte, the 17th-century French chateau where the wedding reception of Tony Parker and Eva Longoria was held.

Tony and Eva honeymooned in the Caribbean. They spent a week on the Turks and Caicos Islands. Then Eva returned to Los Angeles to start production for the new season of *Desperate Housewives*.

Work . . .

Eva Longoria is clearly an ambitious and driven person. Her contract for *Desperate Housewives*, which runs through 2011, pays her more than $9 million per year. Yet she has continued to work on a variety of other projects.

In 2008, Eva starred in another movie, *Over Her Dead Body*. She played a dead woman who haunts the new love interest of

A publicity poster for the 2008 romantic comedy *Over Her Dead Body*. Eva played a deceased woman who haunts the new girlfriend of her former fiancé.

her former fiancé, played by Paul Rudd. Again, Eva's TV star power failed to translate onto the big screen. Many critics panned her performance, and they didn't find the romantic comedy at all funny. Chris Kaltenbach of the *Baltimore Sun* called *Over Her Dead Body* "a hopeless pastiche of timeworn plotlines, hackneyed dialogue and stultifying direction; to call it amateurish is a slap in the face to amateurs everywhere." *Newsday*'s Gene Seymour complained that the movie "makes its 93 minutes seem more like nine hours."

With big-screen stardom continuing to elude her, Eva Longoria formed her own production company, called unbeliEVAble, in 2008. Among its early projects was a one-hour drama for ABC Family TV.

Eva has always loved cooking and food, and in 2008 she partnered with chef and personal friend Todd English to open a Tex-Mex restaurant in Hollywood. The restaurant, called Beso (Spanish for "Kiss"), features two of Eva's favorite recipes, for guacamole and tortilla soup. Eva has said there will always be a table reserved for her cast mates from *Desperate Housewives*.

Eva and Todd English at the March 2008 opening of their Hollywood restaurant, Beso.

Happy couple: The actress and the hoops star enjoy a Spurs victory together. Though she loves her work, Eva Longoria says family is what is most important to her.

. . . and Family

Although she thrives on work, Eva says that family is most important to her. Between the demands of their respective careers, she and Tony Parker spend as much time as they can together at their home in San Antonio. The Spanish-style mansion sits on 23 acres. Fittingly for two people who love sports, the Parkers'

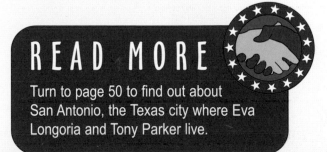

READ MORE

Turn to page 50 to find out about San Antonio, the Texas city where Eva Longoria and Tony Parker live.

With a successful career and a close and loving family, Eva Longoria seems to be living the American dream. "I love life, in general," she has said.

home has an indoor basketball court, beach volleyball and tennis courts, and a mini water park around a large pool.

Most of Eva's family has also moved to San Antonio. Eva loves to sew Halloween costumes for her nieces. She also likes cooking for her family. Eva has repeatedly said that she wants kids, and she might not wait until the end of her contract for *Desperate Housewives*—which expires in 2011 and which she says she will not renew. Her husband, too, is enthusiastic about the idea of becoming a parent. "That would be even better than my NBA titles, even if I don't compare private life and sports," Tony Parker told an interviewer. "Eva talks to me about it all the time. I'd like to have girls, because I come from a world of boys."

Eva Longoria seems to have everything she needs to be happy. "I love my husband with all of my heart," she says, "but I love my family. And I love my girlfriends. And I love my job. And I love my dogs. I love life, in general."

Desperate Housewives

Behind the perfect lives, perfect houses, and perfect lawns on Wisteria Lane live many secrets. *Desperate Housewives*, a prime-time comedy on ABC, premiered on October 3, 2004. It was an immediate hit.

The soap opera housewives are as different as can be. Eva Longoria plays Gabrielle Solis, a former runway model who has an affair with her young gardener. Gaby has a big house and a rich, powerful husband, but what she really wants is true love.

Teri Hatcher plays Susan Mayer, who has married the love of her life. Her life is complicated, however, by the blended family that came with him.

Nicollette Sheridan plays Edie Britt. Edie is a former realtor who has been married and divorced twice. She is highly competitive in work and love.

Felicity Huffman plays Lynette Scavo. Her many challenges revolve around trying to be a super-mom and handle work, health, and family.

Marcia Cross plays Bree Van de Camp. Even as her world crumbles around her, Bree keeps up the façade of a perfect life.

The housewives will continue their adventures at least until 2011, when the stars' current contracts expire.

The women of Wisteria Lane.

CROSS-CURRENTS

Oprah Winfrey

Oprah Winfrey is a talk-show host, an actress, a magazine publisher, and a philanthropist. She has come a long way from her humble beginning.

Oprah was born in rural Mississippi on January 29, 1954, to a poor, unwed teenage mother. Her father was in the army. During her first years, Oprah lived with her grandmother, Hattie Mae Lee, who taught the girl to read when she was three. At the age of six, Oprah moved with her mother from Mississippi to an inner-city neighborhood in Milwaukee, Wisconsin.

At 14, Oprah moved to Tennessee to live with her father. There she landed her first job, at radio station WVOL, while she was in high school. She began to co-anchor the evening news at Nashville's WLAC-TV at 19. She was the youngest news anchor and the first African-American female news anchor at the station.

After eight years in Baltimore as a news co-anchor and co-host of the local talk show, Oprah moved to Chicago to host WLS-TV's morning talk show, *AM Chicago*. The show became the number-one local talk show one month after she began.

Within a year, the show expanded to one hour and was renamed *The Oprah Winfrey Show*. It entered national syndication in 1986, becoming the highest-rated talk show in television history. When her talk show went national, Winfrey became a millionaire at age 32.

Oprah Winfrey.

Quinceañera

A *quinceañera* is a Hispanic celebration marking a 15-year-old girl's passage from childhood into womanhood. The word comes from the Spanish *quince*, meaning "fifteen," and *años*, "years." It is a tradition that dates back to Aztec times, when girls left their families at age 15 to become wives and mothers.

More than a birthday party, the *quinceañera* is a religious and family ceremony that honors Hispanic culture. Family members and friends gather for a celebration that usually includes Mass, dinner, and a dance. The celebration can be as lavish as a wedding.

The *quinceañera* is full of symbolism. During the Mass and at the party, the girl is escorted by her court—14 young couples, *damas* (girls) and *chambelanes* (boys), symbolizing the 14 years of her life. The 15th year is represented by the *quinceañera* herself. She is escorted by her father, and followed by her mother, who is escorted by the girl's *chambelan*.

During the celebration, the girl removes her flat shoes and steps into high heels, to symbolize her "first steps" as a woman. Her father or another paternal figure performs the shoe-changing ritual. There is also a special dance for the father and his daughter. Family members give speeches, share memories of the *quinceañera,* and toast to her health and future happiness.

A *quinceañera*. The traditional rite of passage for Hispanic girls can be as lavish as a wedding.

The Young and the Restless

Since its premiere on March 26, 1973, the daytime soap opera *The Young and the Restless* has been a trend-setting and award-winning program. The show—set in the fictional Genoa City, a center of business—follows the wheeling and dealing, and the romances and tragedies, of its large cast of characters.

In 2008, the program celebrated its 1,000th straight week as the highest-rated daytime soap opera. One reason *Y&R* has dominated in the ratings is its diversity. The show includes African-American, Hispanic, and Asian characters.

Between the writers, producers, cast, and crew, the show has won 100 Emmy Awards, more than any other soap opera. Ten million daily viewers in more than 100 countries watch *Y&R*.

In 2001, Eva Longoria joined the cast as Isabella Braña Williams. After numerous affairs and relationships, Isabella had a son and then married the father of little Ricky, Paul Williams. They eventually divorced.

Isabella attempted to murder Christine Williams, after setting her up for Isabella's faked murder. The night before Christine was to be arrested for Isabella's murder, a very alive Isabella attacked her in her bathtub. Paul arrived in time to save Christine by knocking out Isabella. The police then hauled Isabella to a mental hospital.

After two years of messing with people's lives, Isabella was committed to a mental hospital. Eva Longoria moved to a new show, and *Y&R* continues on.

San Antonio Spurs

In 1967, the American Basketball Association (ABA) was formed as a rival league to the established National Basketball Association (NBA). One of the ABA's original franchises was the Dallas Chaparrals. The franchise relocated to San Antonio in 1973 and was renamed the San Antonio Spurs.

When the ABA dissolved in 1976, the Spurs were one of the four ABA teams that joined the NBA. The Spurs won their first NBA game, over the Philadelphia 76ers, but went more than 20 years before winning a title.

Paced by 7'1" center David Robinson and 6'11" power forward Tim Duncan, San Antonio defeated the New York Knicks, four games to one, to win its first NBA championship in 1999.

In 2003, at the end of Tony Parker's second season with the Spurs, San Antonio captured another title. This time the Spurs beat the New Jersey Nets, four games to two, in the Finals.

In the next four years, the Spurs notched two more NBA championships. In 2005, they won a hard-fought series against the Detroit Pistons. In 2007, they prevailed over the Cleveland Cavaliers. Tony Parker was named MVP of the 2007 Finals.

Tony Parker in action during his rookie season with the San Antonio Spurs, 2001–02.

Eva's Heroes

Eva Longoria's oldest sister, Liza, was born intellectually disabled. While the actress considers herself lucky to have such a wonderful big sister, she also acknowledges the challenges her sibling faces each day.

Eva says Liza is her hero. Liza never sees herself as disabled, and she always sees the good in other people. She has inspired Eva to overcome her own difficulties and disappointments in life.

In 2006, Eva founded a charity to help people like Liza and their families deal with the challenges of their disabilities. Eva's Heroes serves approximately 30 youths and their families. The organization allows intellectually disabled individuals to interact with and learn from their peers without disabilities.

Eva's Heroes is based in San Antonio. Someday, however, Eva hopes to expand the nonprofit program to other locations nationwide.

The ALMA Awards

In Spanish, the word *alma* means "spirit" or "soul." The ALMA (American Latino Media Arts) Awards play off that meaning. The ALMA Awards represent the determined spirit of Latinos and honor positive portrayals of Latinos in film and television. They have been given annually since 1995.

The ALMA Awards show, held every June as a prime-time television special, brings together celebrities and leaders who influence American society. The show is a celebration of Latino heritage and its positive impact on American entertainment and culture. Eva Longoria hosted the ALMA Awards show in 2006, 2007, and 2008.

The ALMA Awards were created by the National Council of La Raza. Founded in 1968, the NCLR is the largest national Latino civil rights and advocacy organization in the United States. Its mission is to improve life opportunities for Hispanic Americans. The NCLR has a network of about 300 community-based partners throughout the country. These groups provide a range of services, including job training, education, and health care.

Eva Longoria at the 2007 ALMA Awards show.

San Antonio

San Antonio is the second-largest city in Texas and the seventh-largest city in the United States. In 2007, the U.S. Census Bureau estimated San Antonio's population at more than 1.3 million.

Twenty million tourists visit San Antonio each year. One of the city's major attractions is the San Antonio River Walk. Shops, restaurants, theaters, and parks follow the course of the waterway as it meanders through downtown San Antonio.

The Alamo, located in the heart of San Antonio, is a historic landmark. For 13 days in early 1836, about 250 supporters of Texas independence—including William Travis, Jim Bowie, and

The Alamo, site of a famous siege in 1836.

Davy Crockett—defended the old mission against a Mexican army numbering some 4,000. The Mexicans were commanded by Antonio López de Santa Anna, Mexico's president. On March 6, the Alamo was overrun and its remaining defenders killed.

"Remember the Alamo" became a rallying cry for the Texas Revolution. On April 21, 1836, Texans commanded by Sam Houston decisively defeated Santa Anna's forces in the battle of San Jacinto, thereby securing independence for Texas. Texas would become a U.S. state less than a decade later, in 1845.

Chronology

1975: Eva Jacqueline Longoria is born on March 15 in Corpus Christi, Texas.

1993: Wins her first beauty pageant competition.

1998: Wins the Miss Corpus Christi USA beauty pageant.

2000: Receives a Bachelor of Science degree in Kinesiology from Texas A&M University–Kingsville.

2000: Lands her first TV role, on *Beverly Hills, 90210.*

2001: Wins role as Isabella Braña Williams on the soap opera *The Young and the Restless.*

2002: Receives an ALMA Award for "Outstanding Actress in a Daytime Drama" for her role as Isabella. Elopes to Las Vegas to marry Tyler Christopher. The marriage lasts two years.

2003: Lands a role in the TV show *L.A. Dragnet.* Is named to *People en Español*'s "Most Beautiful People" list.

2004: Signs contract for starring role as Gabrielle Solis on *Desperate Housewives.* After a San Antonio Spurs basketball game, Eva meets guard Tony Parker.

2005: L'Oréal Paris announces Eva as the new face of L'Oréal. Eva becomes the national spokesperson for PADRES Contra El Cáncer. Eva is named one of the 50 Most Beautiful People by *People en Español*. The actress is nominated for a Golden Globe for "Best Performance by an Actress in a Television Series – Musical or Comedy" for her role on *Desperate Housewives*. Eva wins an ALMA Award for entertainer of the year.

2006: She serves as producer and host of the televised ALMA Awards. As a tribute to her oldest sister, Eva founds a San Antonio-based charity called Eva's Heroes. Eva is named one of the 100 Most Influential Hispanics by *People en Español*. The film *The Sentinel* opens starring Michael Douglas and Eva Longoria. Eva becomes engaged to San Antonio Spurs star Tony Parker.

2007: Eva signs a contract as spokeswoman for Bebe Sportswear. Eva wins "Favorite Female TV Star" for her role on *Desperate Housewives* at the People's Choice Awards. On July 7, Eva marries Tony Parker in Paris. Eva serves as host and executive producer of the 2007 ALMA Awards.

2008: Eva stars in the film *Over Her Dead Body* with Paul Rudd and Jason Biggs. On March 7, Eva opens a Mexican restaurant called Beso with chef Todd English. Eva serves as host and executive producer of the 2008 ALMA Awards. Eva starts her own production company called unbeliEVAble.

Accomplishments/Awards

Television

2000: *Beverly Hills, 90210*

2000: *General Hospital*

2001–2002: *The Young and the Restless*

2003: *L.A. Dragnet*

2004–: *Desperate Housewives*

Films

2003: *Hot Tamales Live: Spicy, Hot and Hilarious*

2004: *Carlita's Secret*

2005: *Harsh Times*

2005: *Hustler's Instinct*

2006: *The Sentinel*

2008: *Foodfight!*

2008: *Over Her Dead Body*

Awards

2002: ALMA Award for "Outstanding Actress in a Daytime Drama" for work in *The Young and the Restless*

2005: Teen Choice Award for "Choice TV Breakout Performance — Female" for *Desperate Housewives*

2006: ALMA Award — "Person of the Year"

2006: Screen Actors Guild Award for "Outstanding Performance by an Ensemble in a Comedy Series" for *Desperate Housewives*

2007: Screen Actors Guild Award for "Outstanding Performance by an Ensemble in a Comedy Series" for *Desperate Housewives*

Bambi Award for "TV Series International" for *Desperate Housewives*

People's Choice Award for "Favorite Female TV Star" for role of Gabrielle Solis on *Desperate Housewives*

Further Reading

Bried, Erin. "Happily Eva After." *Self* (February 2008): 42.

Rojas, Marcela. "The Year of Eva." *Hispanic*, vol. 20, issue 12 (December 2007/January 2008): 66.

Shipnuck, Alan. "Tony & Eva & the Spurs: A Love Story." *Sports Illustrated* vol. 106 (June 27, 2007): 56.

Swartz, Mimi. "Eva Almighty." *Texas Monthly* (September 2007): 162.

Internet Resources

http://www.doloreshuerta.org/dolores_huerta_foundation.htm

The website for one of Eva Longoria's role models and inspirations, activist and labor organizer Dolores Huerta.

http://www.evasheroes.org/

The website for Eva Longoria's charity to help people with developmental disabilities, dedicated to her oldest sister, Liza.

http://www.imdb.com/name/nm0519456

The website of the International Movie Data Base lists films and television programs that Eva Longoria has appeared in and produced.

Publisher's Note: The Web sites listed on this page were active at the time of publication. The publisher is not responsible for Web sites that have changed their address or discontinued operation since the date of publication. The publisher reviews and updates the Web sites each time the book is reprinted.

Glossary

advocacy—active support of a cause, idea, or policy.

franchise—a professional sports team.

kinesiology—the study of how the human body functions and moves.

petite—small and slender in size; dainty.

philanthropist—a person who is generous in assistance to the poor.

quinceañera—a celebration of a Hispanic girl's 15th birthday, marking her passage from childhood to womanhood.

satire—a literary or theatrical work holding up human follies and vices to scorn or ridicule.

soap opera—a television or radio serial program about the daily lives of a group of people, characterized by stock characters and situations, sentimentality, and melodrama.

sultry—sensual and passionate.

Chapter Notes

p. 10: "She's never had a dishwasher . . ." transcript, *The Oprah Winfrey Show*, February 6, 2006.

p. 12: "Oh, no, no, no . . ." Ibid.

p. 12: "And he's like . . ." Ibid.

p. 14: "My first memories . . ." Marcela Rojas, "The Year of Eva," *Hispanic* (December 2007/January 2008): 66.

p. 14: "I grew up in . . ." Mimi Swartz, "Eva Almighty," *Texas Monthly* (September 2007): 257.

p. 15: "I could skin a deer . . ." Stone Phillips, "Longoria: I'm Desperate to Be a Housewife," *Dateline NBC*, October 23, 2005. http://www.msnbc.msn.com/id/9580764/

p. 15: "I was clumsy . . ." Ibid.

p. 17: "I took soap technique . . ." Ibid.

p. 18: "My role on . . ." Kristie Bertucci, "Eva Longoria, Forever Our Chica," *OYE online* (December 14, 2007).

p. 19: You get through it . . ." ." Jeanne Wolf, "I Can Finally Move Forward," *Parade* (November 25, 2007): 5.

p. 20: "because it was such . . ." Swartz, "Eva Almighty," 258.

p. 21: "Let me tell you . . ." Phillips, "Desperate to Be a Housewife."

p. 21: "She hates children . . ." Ibid.

p. 21: "The things we have . . ." Ibid.

p. 22: "I said her dad . . ." Alan Shipnuck, "Tony & Eva & the Spurs: A Love Story," *Sports Illustrated* (June 27, 2007): 56.

p. 25: "just a Mexican . . ." Kevin Hechtkopf, "Longoria, Parker Stopped By Police," *CBS News*, December 26, 2005. http://www.cbsnews.com/stories/2005/12/26/entertainment/main1165392.shtml

p. 28: "It's amazing how . . ." Erin Bried, "Happily Eva After," *Self* (February 2008): 44.

p. 28: "Liza . . . was my hero . . ." *Wolf*, "I Can Finally Move Forward."

p. 28: "It's horrendous . . ." Stephen Armstrong, "I Got Latinos to Vote, but They Voted Religion," *New Statesman* (November 6, 2006).

p. 30: "I take huge . . ." Rojas, *The Year of Eva*, 67.

p. 31: "She's not just . . ." Ibid.

p. 33: "deeply ridiculous, . . ." Stephen Holden, "Michael Douglas as a Secret Service Agent in 'The Sentinel,'" *New York Times*, April 21, 2006. http://movies.nytimes.com/2006/04/21/movies/21sent.html

p. 34: "quite simple, traditional . . ." Lorena Blas, "Wedding Was More Than 'OK'! *USA Today.com*, July 11, 2007. http://www.usatoday.com/life/people/2007-07-10-longoria-parker-OK_N.htm

p. 38: "a hopeless pastiche . . ." Chris Kaltenbach, "'Dead Body' Is Such a Drag," *Baltimore Sun*, February 1, 2008. http://www.baltimoresun.com/entertainment/movies/reviews/bal-to.dead01feb01,0,7664583.story p 38: "makes its 93 minutes . . ." Gene Seymour, review of *Over Her Dead Body*, directed by Jeff Lowell, *Newsday* (February 1, 2008). http://www.newsday.com/entertainment/ny-etsecw5557900feb01,1,4380629.story

p. 41: "That would be . . ." Cesar G. Soriano, "Eva Longoria, Tony Parker Make it Official, Again," *USA Today.com*, July 8, 2007, accessed 5/11/08. http://www.usatoday.com/life/people/2007-07-07-longoria-wedding_N.htm

p. 41: "I love my husband. . ." *Wolf*, "I Can Finally Move Forward," 5.

Index

Numbers in **bold italics** refer to captions.

Photo Credits

About the Author

MARY SCHULTE is a children's book author and newspaper photo editor who lives in Kansas City, Missouri. She is the author of 12 children's books and the mother of three children. She had not watched an episode of *Desperate Housewives* before she began researching this book, but now she's a faithful fan.